# Vegetarian

# Vegetarian

Bounty Books

First published in Great Britain in 1999 by
Hamlyn, a division of Octopus Publishing
Group Ltd

This edition published in 2007 by Bounty Books, a
division of Octopus Publishing Group Ltd
2–4 Heron Quays, London E14 4JP
Reprinted 2008 (twice) , 2009
An Hachette Livre UK Company

ISBN: 978-0-753716-24-3

A CIP catalogue record for this book is available
from the British Library

Printed and bound in China

**Notes**

**1** Standard level spoon measurements are
used in all recipes.

1 tablespoon = one 15 ml spoon
1 teaspoon = one 5 ml spoon

**2** Both imperial and metric measurements
have been given in all recipes. Use one set of
measurements only and not a mixture of both.

**3** Measurements for canned food have been
given as a standard metric equivalent.

**4** Eggs should be medium unless otherwise
stated. The Department of Health advises that
eggs should not be consumed raw. This book
may contain dishes made with lightly cooked
eggs. It is prudent for more vulnerable people,
such as pregnant and nursing mothers,
invalids, the elderly, babies and young
children, to avoid uncooked or lightly cooked
dishes made with eggs. Once prepared, these
dishes should be used immediately.

**5** Milk should be full fat unless otherwise
stated.

**6** Fresh herbs should be used unless
otherwise stated. If unavailable, use dried
herbs as an alternative but halve the
quantities stated.

**7** Pepper should be freshly ground black
pepper unless otherwise stated; season
according to taste.

**8** Ovens should be preheated to the specified
temperature – if using a fan-assisted oven,
follow the manufacturer's instructions for
adjusting the time and the temperature.

**9** Do not refreeze a dish that has been frozen
previously.

**10** This book includes dishes made with nuts
and nut derivatives. It is advisable for
customers with known allergic reactions to
nuts and nut derivatives and those who may
be potentially vulnerable to these allergies,
such as pregnant and nursing mothers,
invalids, the elderly, babies and children, to
avoid dishes made with nuts and nut oils.
It is also prudent to check the labels of
pre-prepared ingredients for the possible
inclusion of nut derivatives.

**11** Vegetarians should look for the 'V' symbol
on a cheese to ensure it is made with
vegetarian rennet. There are vegetarian forms
of Parmesan, feta, Cheddar, Cheshire, red
Leicester, dolcelatte and many goats' cheeses,
among others.

# contents

# 6

# introduction

It has never been so easy to have a varied, interesting and nutritious vegetarian diet. Shops and supermarkets offer an extensive range of fresh produce from all over the world, and storecupboard ingredients – pulses, pasta, grains, nuts and seeds – are now widely available. Delicious vegetarian dishes can be prepared easily and many of them take very little time.

A vegetarian diet is often healthier than one that includes animal products, not least because it is usually lower in saturated fats. There are, however, one or two useful guidelines to ensure that a vegetarian diet is providing all the body's needs.

It is worth knowing that the body cannot absorb iron from vegetables unless vitamin C is present in the meal. This potential problem is easily overcome by ensuring that each meal includes a good selection of different ingredients. A glass of fruit juice, a side salad or some fresh fruit for dessert provides a double-check.

Dairy products, such as milk and cheese, can pose a problem, mainly because they are so easy to incorporate into a meal that busy people may rely too heavily upon them. Although they are good sources of protein, they also have a high fat content, so there is a risk of raising cholesterol levels in the blood. Lower-fat products, such as skimmed or semi-skimmed milk, cottage cheese, curd cheese, low-fat yogurt and fromage frais, may be a wiser choice than full-fat cheeses, double cream and soured cream. As with all foods, a moderate intake is the best approach for healthy eating.

Vegetarians can also be over-reliant on pulses. While it is true that lentils, peas and beans are excellent sources of protein, they lack one amino acid.– a protein 'building block' – that is essential to the body. However, any potential problem is easily solved by combining pulses with grain foods, such as rice, polenta, pasta and, of course, bread. Grains contain the missing amino acid, although they lack two others. Together, pulses and grains provide the complete protein.

The guiding rule with any diet is to include as many different types of food as possible. A balanced vegetarian diet should include fresh vegetables, especially leafy green vegetables, fresh fruit, pulses, grains, bread and potatoes daily. Cheese, oils and fats, dried fruits and nuts should be eaten in moderation. About half of each meal should consist of starchy foods, such as potatoes, pasta or bread. These contain complex carbohydrates which release energy slowly. High in fibre and containing proteins, vitamin B, iron, phosphorus, zinc and other minerals, they are filling, inexpensive, versatile and a pleasure to eat.

There is nothing to compare with the flavour and texture of fresh vegetables, but frozen and canned ones are convenient. Surprisingly, some frozen vegetables contain more nutrients than fresh ones, since there is no long delay between harvesting and delivery to the shop and they have not been on display for any length of time. When buying fresh vegetables, fruit or herbs, avoid any with wilted, yellowing or discoloured leaves, wrinkled, patchy or blackened skins, flaccid stalks or roots, or shrivelled pods. If possible, prepare them immediately before cooking. Prolonged exposure to air or immersion in water spoils the texture and destroys vitamins. The layer just beneath the peel contains the most nutrients, so always peel vegetables, such as potatoes and carrots, as thinly as possible. Minimum cooking preserves colour and nutrients – and the vegetables taste better. As a rule, leafy and salad vegetables can be stored in the salad drawer of the refrigerator for a few days, but fresh is always the best option. Most root vegetables can be stored in a cool, dark place for up to two weeks. Always unwrap pre-packed vegetables before storing them.

Most dried pulses need pre-soaking, preferably overnight, although some, such as red lentils, do not. Boil dried pulses vigorously for at least 10 minutes to destroy any naturally occurring toxins, then simmer gently until tender. Canned varieties do not need to be boiled in this way.

Buy nuts and seeds in fairly small quantities as they turn rancid quite rapidly. Packed with nutrients, they are immensely useful, providing flavour, colour and texture to all kinds of dishes and make an attractive garnish. For the best flavour, lightly roast or dry-fry before use.

Unless specifically labelled 'vegetarian', margarine may contain animal products, like skimmed milk or whey, although it is predominantly made from refined vegetable oils. Butter, margarine and other spreads contain more or less the same number of calories and the same amount of fat, unless labelled 'low-fat' or 'reduced fat'. Sunflower and olive spreads are higher in polyunsaturated and monounsaturated fats, which are healthier than saturated fats. Margarine containing palm oil or coconut oil is high in saturated fat. Remember that some fat is essential for nutrition, but it should not constitute more than one-third of the day's calorie intake.

Vegetarian cheese is made without using animal rennet for separating the curds and whey. An increasing number of varieties is becoming available.

The recipes featured in this book are designed to help you create enjoyable, as well as nutritious vegetarian dishes. In some, individual vegetables play the leading role, while in others, the flavours of the ingredients blend together and mingle deliciously. Do not be afraid to experiment, substituting seasonal vegetables for those suggested in the recipe or by trying different herbs and spices.

# 'The English only have three vegetables – and two of them are cabbage.'

Walter Page

# basic recipes

# pasta dough

Making fresh pasta is much easier with the aid of a pasta machine, a great investment for pasta lovers.

1 Sift the flour and salt into a bowl, make a well in the centre and gradually work in the eggs, egg yolk, oil and enough water to form a soft dough.

2 Turn out on to a lightly floured surface and knead for 5 minutes until the dough is smooth and elastic. Brush with a little oil, cover and leave to rest for 30 minutes.

3 Divide the dough into 8 pieces. Take one piece and pat into a flattish rectangle. With the pasta rolling machine set at its widest setting, feed the dough through twice. Repeat the process at each setting, feeding the sheet of dough through the rollers lengthways, until the sheet is long and very thin. Cut the sheet in half widthways and hang over a pole to dry for 5 minutes. Repeat with the remaining pieces of dough to make 16 sheets of pasta.

250 g (8 oz) pasta flour or strong white bread flour, plus extra for dusting

1 teaspoon salt

2 eggs, plus 1 egg yolk

1 tablespoon extra virgin olive oil, plus extra for brushing

1–2 tablespoons cold water

**Makes 16 sheets**

**Preparation time:** 20 minutes, plus resting

# classic cheese sauce

1 Put the milk, onion and bay leaf in a pan and heat until just boiling. Remove from the heat, set aside for 20 minutes. Strain and set aside.

2 Melt the butter in a pan, stir in the flour and cook over a low heat for 1 minute. Remove from the heat and beat in the milk, a little at a time, until blended. Return to a low heat and stir constantly until the sauce has thickened. Bring to a gentle boil, stirring; simmer for 2 minutes.

3 Remove the pan from the heat and stir in the Cheddar or Gruyère cheese. Season with salt and pepper.

600 ml (1 pint) milk

1 small onion, roughly chopped

1 bay leaf

50 g (2 oz) butter

50 g (2 oz) plain flour

125 g (4 oz) Cheddar or Gruyère cheese, grated

salt and pepper

| **Makes about 600 ml (1 pint)** |
| **Preparation time:** 25 minutes |
| **Cooking time:** 8–10 minutes |

# crispy basil

This is an attractive garnish with a twist. You can make Crispy Mint in the same way using 25 g (1 oz) mint leaves.

1 Heat the oil in a wok until it is hot, add the basil and chilli and stir-fry for 1 minute until crispy. Remove with a slotted spoon and drain on kitchen paper.

2 tablespoons groundnut oil

25 g (1 oz) basil leaves

1 small red chilli, finely sliced

| **Preparation time:** 2 minutes |
| **Cooking time:** 1 minute |

# just for starters

1 onion, roughly chopped

2 garlic cloves, crushed

1 kg (2 lb) root vegetables (carrots, leeks, parsnips, swede), roughly chopped

4 tablespoons extra virgin olive oil

2 teaspoons clear honey

4 thyme sprigs

4 rosemary sprigs

2 bay leaves

4 ripe tomatoes, quartered

1.2 litres (2 pints) vegetable stock or water

salt and pepper

**To Serve:**

French bread, toasted

Rouille (see page 17)

**Serves 4–6**

**Preparation time:** 15 minutes

**Cooking time:** 1¼ hours

1 In a bowl, toss the onion, garlic and root vegetables with the oil and honey and place in a roasting tin. Add the herbs and place in a preheated oven, 200°C (400°F) Gas Mark 6, for 25 minutes. Add the tomatoes and roast for 25 minutes more. Reduce the oven temperature to 190°C (375°F) Gas Mark 5.

2 Discard the herbs and put the vegetables into a blender or food processor. Add half the stock or water and process until smooth. Blend in the remaining stock or water. Transfer to a casserole, season to taste and bake for 20 minutes. Serve with toasted French bread and rouille.

# oven-baked soup

# green bean & vegetable soup with pesto

1 Heat the oil in a large saucepan and fry the leek and garlic, stirring occasionally, for 5 minutes. Add the potato, celery and thyme and fry, stirring frequently, for a further 10 minutes until light golden.

2 Stir in the flageolet beans with their liquid and the vegetable stock or water, bring to the boil, cover and simmer gently for 20 minutes. Add the courgette, French beans and broad beans and cook for a further 10 minutes. Season to taste.

3 Ladle the soup into large bowls. Stir in a spoonful of pesto into each one and serve with French bread and Parmesan, if wished.

■ Pesto is an Italian sauce made from basil, pine nuts, olive oil and Parmesan cheese. Ready-made varieties are widely available from supermarkets and delicatessens.

2 tablespoons extra virgin olive oil

1 leek, sliced

2 garlic cloves, crushed

1 potato, diced

1 celery stick, sliced

1 tablespoon chopped thyme

1 x 425 g (14 oz) can flageolet beans

600 ml (1 pint) vegetable stock or water

1 courgette, diced

50 g (2 oz) French beans, halved

125 g (4 oz) broad beans

4 teaspoons ready-made pesto sauce

salt and pepper

**To Serve:**

French bread

freshly grated vegetarian Parmesan cheese (optional)

**Serves 4–6**

**Preparation time:** 15 minutes

**Cooking time:** 1¼ hours

# chickpea, pasta & spinach soup

1 Heat the oil in a large saucepan and fry the garlic, onion and rosemary over a low heat for 5 minutes until softened but not golden. Add the chickpeas with their liquid and the vegetable stock or water, bring to the boil, cover and simmer for 30 minutes.

2 Add the pasta, return to the boil and simmer for 6–8 minutes.

3 Meanwhile, make the croûtons heat the olive oil in a frying pan. When the oil is hot, add the bread cubes and stir-fry for 2–3 minutes until golden on all sides. Remove from the frying pan with a slotted spoon and drain thoroughly on kitchen paper.

4 Stir the spinach into the soup and continue cooking for a further 5 minutes until both the pasta and spinach are tender. Season to taste and serve at once, sprinkled with croûtons, nutmeg and Parmesan.

**Soup:**

2 tablespoons extra virgin olive oil

2 garlic cloves, crushed

1 onion, chopped

1 tablespoon chopped rosemary

2 x 425 g (14 oz) cans chickpeas

1.2 litres (2 pints) vegetable stock or water

75 g (3 oz) small pasta shapes

125 g (4 oz) spinach leaves, shredded

salt and pepper

**Croûtons:**

4 tablespoons extra virgin olive oil

4 thick slices day-old bread, crusts removed and cut into cubes

**To Serve:**

freshly grated nutmeg

freshly grated vegetarian Parmesan cheese

**Serves 6**

**Preparation time:** 10 minutes

**Cooking time:** 45 minutes

3 tablespoons olive oil

2 onions, chopped

6 small leeks, diced

4 carrots, diced

6 garlic cloves, sliced

375 g (12 oz) salad leaves, such as watercress, young spinach leaves, mustard greens, parsley or sorrel, very finely chopped

1.5 litres (2½ pints) vegetable stock or water

5 tablespoons ready-made pesto

salt and pepper

**To Garnish:**

watercress or parsley sprigs

| | |
|---|---|
| **Serves 10** | |
| **Preparation time:** 20 minutes | |
| **Cooking time:** 25–30 minutes | |

1 Heat the olive oil in a large saucepan. Fry the onions, leeks, carrots and garlic over a gentle heat, stirring occasionally, for 5 minutes until softened.

2 Stir in the salad leaves and cook, stirring, until they have wilted. Pour in the stock or water, bring to the boil, then simmer gently for about 25 minutes.

3 Season to taste with salt and pepper, then stir in the pesto and heat through. Serve in warmed bowls and garnish with watercress or parsley sprigs.

# green vegetable soup with pesto

# vegetable platter with rouille

1 First make the rouille. Put the red pepper, garlic, chillies and olive oil into a blender or food processor and process until fairly smooth. Scrape down the sides of the bowl with a spatula occasionally to make sure you blend all the ingredients evenly. Add the breadcrumbs and salt and pepper to taste, and process again to form a thick paste. Transfer to a small bowl, cover and chill until ready to serve.

2 Prepare the vegetables according to type and size – the dish will look more attractive if all the vegetables are of a similar size, or are cut into similar-sized pieces. Boil or steam the vegetables until just tender. Drain and refresh under cold running water, then drain again thoroughly.

3 Arrange the vegetables on a large serving platter. Drizzle with olive oil and sprinkle with sea salt. Serve with the rouille and garnish with torn mint leaves.

**Vegetable Platter:**

selection of vegetables, such as carrots, baby fennel, sea kale and baby turnips

extra virgin olive oil

sea salt

**Rouille:**

1 red pepper, cored, deseeded and chopped

2 garlic cloves, chopped

2 red chillies, cored, deseeded and chopped

6 tablespoons extra virgin olive oil

25 g (1 oz) fresh white breadcrumbs

salt and pepper

**To Garnish:**

mint leaves

| Serves 4–6 |
| --- |
| **Preparation time:** 30 minutes |
| **Cooking time:** 20–30 minutes |

2 tablespoons vegetable oil

1 onion, chopped

2 celery sticks, chopped

2 small carrots, chopped

2 x 425 g (14 oz) cans chopped tomatoes

300 ml (½ pint) vegetable stock or water

500 g (1 lb) frozen raspberries, thawed and sieved

2 tablespoons lemon juice

2 tablespoons caster sugar (optional)

salt and pepper

**To Garnish:**

handful of raspberries

150 ml (¼ pint) natural yogurt

1   Heat the oil in a large saucepan. Fry the onion, celery and carrots for 5 minutes until softened. Add the tomatoes and vegetable stock or water and season with pepper. Bring to the boil, then simmer for 15 minutes.

2   Add the raspberry purée, lemon juice and sugar, if using. Taste and adjust the seasoning if necessary. Turn the mixture into a blender or food processor and process until smooth.

3   To serve, heat the soup through, then pour into warmed bowls and garnish each one with raspberries and a spoonful of yogurt.

| |
|---|
| **Serves 6** |
| **Preparation time:** 20 minutes |
| **Cooking time:** 20 minutes |

# fruity tomato soup

# leek & filo parcels

1 Melt half the butter or margarine in a frying pan and gently fry the leeks and garlic for 4–5 minutes until the leeks are tender. Leave to cool slightly, then stir in the crème fraîche or fromage frais, chervil and nutmeg and season with salt and pepper.

2 Melt the remaining butter or margarine in another pan, add the breadcrumbs and stir-fry for 4–5 minutes until golden. Stir into the leek mixture with the Parmesan.

3 Cut each sheet of pastry length-ways into 3 strips. Brush 1 strip with oil, place a second on top and brush again (keep the remaining sheets covered with a damp tea towel to prevent the pastry from drying out). Place a heaped tablespoon of the leek mixture at one end of the filo pastry. Fold over on the diagonal and con-tinue folding along the length of the pastry to enclose the filling. Brush with oil and transfer to an oiled baking sheet. Repeat to make 12 triangles.

4 Bake in a preheated oven, 200°C (400°F) Gas Mark 6, for 20–25 minutes until golden. Serve with extra crème fraîche and garnish with chervil.

40 g (1½ oz) butter or vegetarian margarine

500 g (1 lb) leeks, thinly sliced

1 garlic clove, crushed

4 tablespoons crème fraîche or fromage frais, plus extra to serve

1 tablespoon chopped chervil

freshly grated nutmeg

25 g (1 oz) fresh white breadcrumbs

25 g (1 oz) vegetarian Parmesan cheese, grated

8 large sheets filo pastry, thawed if frozen

extra virgin olive oil, for brushing

salt and pepper

**To Garnish:**

chervil sprigs

| Serves 4–6 |
| --- |
| **Preparation time:** 15 minutes |
| **Cooking time:** 30–35 minutes |

# fava

1  Put the split peas in a saucepan and add enough cold water to cover the peas by about 2.5 cm (1 inch). Bring to the boil and simmer over a low heat, stirring frequently, for 30–35 minutes until all the water is absorbed and the peas are cooked. Leave to cool slightly.

2  Place the peas in a liquidizer with all the remaining ingredients, season with salt and pepper to taste, and process until smooth, adding 2–3 tablespoons of boiling water if the mixture is too thick.

3  Transfer to a serving dish and sprinkle with the parsley and cayenne. Drizzle with olive oil. Serve with a selection of prepared raw vegetables and warm pitta bread for dipping.

50 g (2 oz) yellow split peas, rinsed

4 tablespoons extra virgin olive oil

1 small garlic clove, crushed

1 tablespoon lemon juice

¼ teaspoon ground cumin

½ teaspoon mustard powder

pinch of cayenne pepper

salt and pepper

**To Garnish:**

1 tablespoon chopped parsley

pinch of cayenne pepper

1 tablespoon extra virgin olive oil

**To Serve:**

prepared raw vegetables

warm pitta bread

**Serves 4**

**Preparation time:** 5 minutes

**Cooking time:** 40–45 minutes

This puréed bean paste is similar to hummus, but is made with yellow split peas. It is a Greek dish, served as a dip as part of a meze (a selection of little appetizers).

egg noodles with oyster mushrooms ●

mozzarella & plum tomato lasagne with chilli ●

vegetarian cannelloni ●

baked pasta with aubergine & pepper ●

fusilli with cauliflower & hazelnuts ●

beetroot ravioli with dill cream ●

tagliatelle with tomato & basil sauce ●

grandmother's baked pasta ●

wild mushroom lasagne ●

mushroom ravioli ●

barley bake with squash & mushrooms ●

butternut squash risotto ●

yellow rice with mushrooms ●

baby vegetable stir-fry with orange & soy sauce ●

borlotti bean goulash ●

bean & mushroom salad ●

braised vegetables with mozzarella & tomato ●

# classic
# dishes

200 g (7 oz) dried egg noodles

2 tablespoons groundnut oil

3 garlic cloves, chopped

1 teaspoon sugar

1 tablespoon soy sauce

1 tablespoon vegetarian fish sauce

½ teaspoon salt

50 g (2 oz) oyster mushrooms, torn

½ onion, chopped

125 g (4 oz) mangetout, topped and tailed

4 large orange chillies, sliced lengthways into julienne strips

pepper

1 Cook the noodles in boiling water for 5–6 minutes. Drain and rinse in cold water to stop further cooking.

2 Heat the oil in a preheated wok, add the garlic, then the noodles, sugar, soy sauce, fish sauce and salt. Stir vigorously over a high heat for 1 minute.

3 Add the mushrooms, onion, mangetout and chillies and cook, tossing and stirring constantly, for 2–3 minutes, then lower the heat and check the seasoning. Transfer to a dish and serve at once.

| | |
|---|---|
| **Serves 2–3** | |
| **Preparation time:** 5 minutes | |
| **Cooking time:** 10–12 minutes | |

# egg noodles with oyster mushrooms

1 Grease a rectangular 1.2 litre (2 pint) ovenproof dish and line it with 2 sheets of lasagne, cutting them to fit if necessary. Slice 6 of the tomatoes and arrange half the slices over the lasagne, packing them in well. Sprinkle with salt and add a few slices of mozzarella and goats' cheese and some oregano. Lay 2 more lasagne sheets on top and cover with the remaining tomato slices, half the remaining cheese slices and the remaining oregano. Top with the 2 remaining lasagne sheets.

2 Cut the remaining tomatoes into wedges, and scatter them over the pasta with the remaining cheese. Drizzle with the chilli-flavoured oil and cook in a preheated oven, 200°C (400°F) Gas Mark 6, for 20–30 minutes. Remove from the oven and leave to rest for 10 minutes before serving.

butter or vegetarian margarine, for greasing

6 no pre-cook sheets lasagne verde

10 large plum tomatoes

125 g (4 oz) mozzarella cheese, sliced

1 x 125 g (4 oz) vegetarian goats' cheese, sliced

1 small bunch oregano, chopped

a few drops of chilli-flavoured oil

salt

| Serves 4 |
| --- |
| **Preparation time:** 10 minutes |
| **Cooking time:** 20–30 minutes |

# mozzarella & plum tomato lasagne with chilli

# vegetarian cannelloni

1 Grease a 1.8 litre (3 pint) oven-proof dish. Heat the oil in a large frying pan and fry the onion, celery and carrot for 1 minute. Stir in the oregano and tarragon, then cover the pan and cook over a low heat for 10 minutes, adding a splash of water if they appear a little dry.

2 Stir in the flageolet beans, mushroom sauce and kale. Season with salt and pepper and simmer for a further 10 minutes.

3 Spoon the filling into the cannelloni tubes with a teaspoon and arrange them in the prepared dish. Add the cream, if using, to the remaining vegetable mixture to soften it, and pour it over the pasta.

4 Beat together the ricotta or mascarpone, eggs and Parmesan and season well. Spread this mixture over the pasta and cook in a preheated oven, 180°C (350°F) Gas Mark 4, for 45 minutes, covering with foil if over-browning.

butter or vegetarian margarine, for greasing

1 tablespoon oil

1 onion, chopped

2 celery sticks, very finely sliced

1 carrot, finely chopped

1 tablespoon oregano

1 tablespoon tarragon

1 x 400 g (13 oz) can flageolet beans

1 x 375 g (12 oz) carton fresh mushroom sauce

125 g (4 oz) baby curly kale, shredded

10 cannelloni tubes

150 ml (¼ pint) single cream (optional)

250 g (8 oz) ricotta or mascarpone cheese

2 eggs, beaten

3 tablespoons freshly grated vegetarian Parmesan cheese

salt and pepper

| Serves 4–6 |
| --- |
| **Preparation time:** 20 minutes |
| **Cooking time:** 1 hour 10 minutes |

# baked pasta with aubergine & pepper

1 Heat half the oil in a large frying pan and stir-fry the aubergine over a medium heat for 6–8 minutes until golden and tender. Remove with a slotted spoon. Add the remaining oil and stir-fry the onion, peppers and oregano for 10 minutes.

2 Bring a large pan of water to a rolling boil, add 1 teaspoon salt and the pasta. Return to the boil and simmer for 10–12 minutes until the pasta is tender, but still firm to the bite. Drain and toss with the tomato sauce and vegetables. Season to taste. Spoon into a deep, oiled, 20 x 30 cm (8 x 12 inch) ovenproof dish.

3 Beat together the remaining ingredients and pour over the pasta mixture. Bake in a preheated oven, 180°C (350°F) Gas Mark 4, for 35–40 minutes until the topping is set and golden. Leave to stand for 5 minutes, then serve with a mixed salad.

■ Make a quick tomato sauce by mixing 2 x 425 g/14 oz cans chopped tomatoes, 2 garlic cloves, 2 tablespoons each olive oil and chopped basil. Season and simmer for 10 minutes.

4 tablespoons extra virgin olive oil

1 large aubergine, diced

1 onion, chopped

2 red peppers, cored, deseeded and diced

1 tablespoon dried oregano

175 g (6 oz) dried penne

1 quantity Quick Tomato Sauce (see below)

2 egg yolks

250 ml (8 fl oz) crème fraîche or fromage frais

2 tablespoons milk

125 g (4 oz) vegetarian feta cheese, diced

salt and pepper

**To Serve:**

mixed salad

**Serves 4–6**

**Preparation time:** 1 hour 20 minutes

**Cooking time:** 50 minutes

# fusilli with cauliflower & hazelnuts

1 Melt the butter or margarine in a frying pan and stir-fry the breadcrumbs and hazelnuts over a medium heat for about 3 minutes until crisp and golden. Drain on kitchen paper and set aside.

2 Bring a large pan of water to a rolling boil, add 1 teaspoon salt and the pasta. Return to the boil and cook over a medium heat for 10–12 minutes until the pasta is tender, but still firm to the bite.

3 Meanwhile, heat half the oil in a pan and fry the cauliflower, garlic and chilli for 8–10 minutes until the cauliflower is golden. Add the parsley.

4 Drain the pasta, toss with the remaining oil and season to taste. Stir the pasta into the cauliflower mixture. Serve topped with the breadcrumb mixture.

25 g (1 oz) butter or vegetarian margarine

50 g (2 oz) fresh white breadcrumbs

25 g (1 oz) hazelnuts, finely chopped

375 g (12 oz) dried fusilli

8 tablespoons hazelnut oil

1 cauliflower, divided into small florets

2 garlic cloves, sliced

1 dried red chilli, deseeded and chopped

2 tablespoons chopped parsley

salt and pepper

**Serves 4**

**Preparation time:** 15 minutes

**Cooking time:** 15–18 minutes

▓ Fusilli is the spiral or corkscrew-shaped pasta; macaroni or farfalle could be used instead. Broccoli makes a tasty alternative to cauliflower and is particularly good when 50 g (2 oz) sultanas are added along with the parsley.

# beetroot ravioli with dill cream

1 Make the pasta dough, following steps 1 and 2 of the recipe, see page 8. Wrap in clingfilm and set aside.

2 For the filling, heat the oil in a frying pan and fry the onion and caraway seeds over a medium heat for 5 minutes until golden. Add the beetroot and cook for 5 minutes. Put the mixture in a food processor or blender and process until smooth. Leave to cool, then beat in the remaining filling ingredients. Season to taste.

3 Following step 3 of the pasta recipe, roll out the dough to form 8 sheets and cut each in half widthways. Lay one sheet on a floured surface and place 5 heaped teaspoons of the filling at 2.5 cm (1 inch) intervals over the dough. Dampen around the mounds of filling with a wet pastry brush and lay a second sheet of pasta over the top, pressing around the mounds to seal. Cut into round ravioli using a cutter or into squares using a sharp knife and place on a floured tea towel. Repeat to make 40 ravioli.

4 Cook the ravioli in a large pan of lightly salted boiling water for 3–4 minutes or until tender. Meanwhile, make the dill cream. Heat the oil in a small saucepan, add the dill and green peppercorns and remove from the heat. Stir in the crème fraîche. Drain the ravioli well, transfer to a warm serving dish and toss with the dill cream. Serve at once.

1 quantity Pasta Dough (see page 8)

**Filling:**

1 tablespoon extra virgin olive oil

1 small onion, finely chopped

½ teaspoon caraway seeds

175 g (6 oz) cooked beetroot, chopped

175 g (6 oz) ricotta or curd cheese

25 g (1 oz) dried breadcrumbs

1 egg yolk

2 tablespoons freshly grated vegetarian Parmesan cheese

grated nutmeg

salt and pepper

**Dill Cream:**

4 tablespoons walnut oil

4 tablespoons chopped dill

1 tablespoon drained green peppercorns in brine, crushed

6 tablespoons crème fraîche or fromage frais

**Serves 4–6**

**Preparation time:** 1 hour

**Cooking time:** 22–25 minutes

1 Heat 3 tablespoons of the olive oil in a large frying pan and gently fry the onions and garlic over a low heat, stirring occasionally, until soft and slightly coloured.

2 Add the tomatoes, tomato purée, sugar and wine, stirring well. Cook over a gentle heat until the mixture is quite thick and reduced. Stir in the olives and basil leaves and season to taste with salt and pepper.

3 Meanwhile, bring a large pan of water to a rolling boil, add 1 teaspoon salt, 1 tablespoon of the remaining oil and the pasta. Return to the boil and cook over a medium heat for 10–12 minutes until the pasta is tender, but still firm to the bite.

4 Drain the tagliatelle, mixing in the remaining olive oil and plenty of pepper. Mix the pasta with the tomato sauce and serve with large curls of shaved Parmesan cheese.

5 tablespoons olive oil

2 onions, chopped

2 garlic cloves, crushed

500 g (1 lb) plum tomatoes, skinned and chopped

2 tablespoons tomato purée

1 teaspoon sugar

100 ml (3½ fl oz) dry white wine

few ripe olives, pitted and quartered

25 g (1 oz) basil leaves, torn

375 g (12 oz) dried tagliatelle

salt and pepper

**To Garnish:**

vegetarian Parmesan cheese shavings

**Serves 4**

**Preparation time:** 10 minutes

**Cooking time:** 20 minutes

# tagliatelle with tomato & basil sauce

# grandmother's baked pasta

1 Bring at least 1.8 litres (3 pints) water to the boil in a large saucepan. Add the oil and 1 teaspoon salt. Add the pasta and cook for 6 minutes until nearly tender. Drain well and return to the saucepan with the cream and Parmesan and stir to combine.

2 Arrange half the tomatoes in a large ovenproof dish, dot with half the butter or margarine and sprinkle with half the basil. Season with salt and pepper. Arrange the pasta on top, then cover with the remaining basil and tomatoes. Dot with the remaining butter or margarine and season with salt and pepper.

3 Bake, uncovered, in a preheated oven, 200°C (400°F) Gas Mark 6, for about 30 minutes. Garnish with basil sprigs. Serve immediately.

1 tablespoon olive oil

375 g (12 oz) dried fusilli

300 ml (½ pint) double cream

75 g (3 oz) freshly grated vegetarian Parmesan cheese

875 g (1¾ lb) juicy, ripe tomatoes, thinly sliced

50 g (2 oz) butter or vegetarian margarine

small bunch of basil, leaves torn

salt and pepper

**To Garnish:**

sprigs of basil

| Serves 4 |
| --- |
| **Preparation time:** 10 minutes |
| **Cooking time:** 36 minutes |

# wild mushroom lasagne

1 Place the dried ceps in a bowl and pour over the boiling water. Leave to soak for 30 minutes, then drain, reserving the liquid. Slice the ceps.

2 Heat the oil in a large frying pan and fry the shallots, garlic and thyme for 5 minutes. Add the ceps and fresh mushrooms and fry for 5 minutes until golden. Add the wine and boil for 5 minutes. Add the tomatoes, sun-dried tomatoes, reserved soaking liquid and soy sauce, bring to the boil and simmer gently for 15 minutes. Season to taste.

3 Assemble the lasagne. Pour one-third of the mushrooms into a 20 x 25 cm (8 x 10 inch) ovenproof dish and top with 4 sheets of lasagne, one-third of the cheese sauce and one-third of the mozzarella. Repeat with the remaining ingredients, finishing with a layer of cheese sauce and mozzarella.

4 Bake the mushroom lasagne in a preheated oven, 190°C (375°F) Gas 5, for about 45 minutes until it is bubbling and golden.

15 g (½ oz) dried ceps

150 ml (¼ pint) boiling water

3 tablespoons extra virgin olive oil

4 shallots, chopped

2 garlic cloves, chopped

1 tablespoon chopped thyme

750 g (1½ lb) mixed cultivated mushrooms

150 ml (¼ pint) dry white wine

500 g (1 lb) tomatoes, skinned and chopped or 1 x 425 g (14 oz) can chopped tomatoes

50 g (2 oz) drained sun-dried tomatoes in oil, chopped

1 tablespoon dark soy sauce

12 sheets pre-cooked lasagne or fresh lasagne

1 quantity Classic Cheese Sauce (see page 9)

250 g (8 oz) mozzarella cheese

salt and pepper

**Serves 6**

**Preparation time:** 40 minutes, plus soaking, plus making sauce

**Cooking time:** 40–45 minutes

■ Wild mushrooms or ceps tend to be expensive, but you will only need a very small quantity. This recipe also uses cultivated mushrooms, such as oyster and shiitake mushrooms, available in most large supermarkets.

vegetarian

# mushroom ravioli

1 Make the pasta dough, following steps 1 and 2 of the recipe, see page 8. Wrap in clingfilm and set aside.

2 Heat the oil and gently fry the onion and garlic until soft and lightly coloured. Add the mushrooms and continue to cook gently until the mushrooms are soft and any liquid has evaporated. Remove from the heat, beat in the ricotta and egg and sufficient breadcrumbs to give a firm mixture. Season to taste.

3 Following step 3 of the pasta recipe, roll out the dough to form 8 sheets and cut each in half widthways. Cut out 6 cm (2½ inch) rounds. Place a portion of the mixture on each, brush around the edge of the dough with cold water, fold over and seal. Alternatively, cut out 2.5 cm (1 inch) square or round shapes, place the filling in the centre, brush around the edge of the dough with cold water, top with a matching shape and seal.

4 Cook a few ravioli at a time for 4–5 minutes in boiling salted water. They are cooked when they rise to the surface. Remove with a slotted spoon, drain well and place in a hot serving dish. Cover and keep hot until all the ravioli are cooked. Just before serving, heat the butter or margarine in a pan until it is a light golden brown and immediately pour it over the ravioli. Sprinkle a little of the Parmesan over the top and serve, handing the remaining Parmesan separately.

2 tablespoons olive oil

1 onion, finely chopped

1–2 garlic cloves, crushed

500 g (1 lb) mushrooms, finely chopped

200 g (7 oz) ricotta cheese

1 egg, beaten

2–3 tablespoons white breadcrumbs

1 x quantity Pasta Dough (see page 8)

75 g (3 oz) butter or vegetarian margarine

50 g (2 oz) vegetarian Parmesan cheese, grated

salt and pepper

**Serves 4**

**Preparation time:** 1 hour

**Cooking time:** 30 minutes

# barley bake with squash & mushrooms

1 Rinse the barley for several minutes under cold running water, drain well and shake dry. Place in a saucepan, pour over the boiling stock and bring back to the boil. Cover the pan and simmer gently for 40 minutes until the stock is absorbed and the barley tender.

2 Melt the butter or margarine in a frying pan and gently fry the onion, stirring occasionally, for 5 minutes until soft, but not browned. Add the squash, mushrooms and rosemary to the pan and fry for a further 5 minutes. Stir the mixture into the barley with the remaining ingredients until evenly combined.

3 Grease an ovenproof dish, transfer the barley mixture to it and bake in a preheated oven, 200°C (400°F) Gas Mark 6, for 20 minutes until golden and bubbling. Garnish with chopped parsley and serve immediately with a mixed salad.

175 g (6 oz) pearl barley

600 ml (1 pint) boiling vegetable stock

25 g (1 oz) butter or vegetarian margarine, plus extra for greasing

1 onion, sliced

500 g (1 lb) peeled squash, cubed

250 g (8 oz) shiitake or button mushrooms, halved if large

2 tablespoons chopped rosemary

½ teaspoon cayenne pepper

1 x 200 g (7 oz) can chopped tomatoes

150 ml (¼ pint) single cream

50 g (2 oz) vegetarian Gruyère or Cheddar cheese, grated

salt and pepper

**To Garnish:**

chopped parsley

**To Serve:**

mixed salad

**Serves 4–6**

**Preparation time:** 25 minutes

**Cooking time:** 1 hour

# butternut squash risotto

1 Top and tail the squash, cut in half around the middle, then pare away the skin from one half without losing too much of the flesh. Cut in half lengthways, remove the seeds and cut into 5 cm (2 inch) dice. Repeat with the other half. Place on a large baking sheet, drizzle with 2 tablespoons of the olive oil and season with salt and pepper. Mix well and cook in the top of a preheated oven, 220°C (425°F) Gas Mark 7, for 15 minutes until softened and slightly browned.

2 Meanwhile, heat the stock to a gentle simmer in a saucepan.

3 Melt the remaining olive oil and 50 g (2 oz) of the butter or margarine in a heavy-based saucepan and gently fry the garlic and onion, without browning, for 5 minutes. Add the rice, stirring well to coat the grains with oil and butter or margarine, then add enough stock to cover. Stir well and simmer gently. Continue to stir frequently. As the liquid is absorbed, continue adding ladles of stock to just cover the rice.

4 Remove the squash from the oven, add to the risotto with the Parmesan and the remaining butter or margarine, season with salt and pepper and stir gently. Serve the risotto on warmed plates drizzled with a little pumpkin seed oil.

1 butternut squash, weighing 1 kg (2 lb)

3 tablespoons olive oil

1 litre (1¾ pints) vegetable stock

125 g (4 oz) butter or vegetarian margarine

1 garlic clove, crushed and chopped

1 onion, finely diced

300 g (10 oz) arborio rice

150 g (5 oz) vegetarian Parmesan cheese, freshly grated

salt and pepper

**To Serve:**

pumpkin seed oil

**Serves 4**

**Preparation time:** 5 minutes

**Cooking time:** 25 minutes

2 tablespoons groundnut oil

500 g (l lb) cooked rice

125 g (4 oz mangetout, topped and tailed

125 g (4 oz) button mushrooms, halved

125 g (4 oz) drained canned bamboo shoots

1 teaspoon ground turmeric

2 teaspoons sugar

1 tablespoon soy sauce

1 teaspoon salt

pepper

**To Garnish:**

1 tablespoon fried garlic slices

1 large red chilli, deseeded and cut into strips

**Serves 2–3**

**Preparation time:** 3 minutes

**Cooking time:** 3–4 minutes

1 Heat the oil in a preheated wok. Add the rice and give it a good stir, then add the rest of the ingredients. Stir-fry over a low heat until thoroughly mixed. Increase the heat and stir and toss for 1–2 minutes, making sure the rice does not stick to the wok.

2 Serve in warmed bowls and garnish with the fried garlic slices and chilli.

# yellow rice with mushrooms

# baby vegetable stir-fry with orange & soy sauce

1 Prepare the sauce. Blend the corn-flour in a jug with the cold water, then add the orange rind and juice, the soy sauce and rice wine or sherry. Stir well to combine.

2 Heat an empty wok until hot. Add the oil and heat until hot. Add the carrots and baby corn and stir-fry for 5 minutes, then add the mushrooms and stir-fry for 3–4 minutes.

3 Pour in the sauce mixture and bring to the boil over a high heat, stirring constantly until thickened and glossy. Add salt and pepper to taste. Garnish with coriander leaves and serve with egg noodles.

2 tablespoons groundnut oil

175 g (6 oz) baby carrots

175 g (6 oz) baby corn

175 g (6 oz) small button mushrooms

salt and pepper

**Sauce:**

2 teaspoons cornflour

4 tablespoons cold water

finely grated rind and juice of 1 large orange

2 tablespoons soy sauce

1 tablespoon rice wine or dry sherry

**To Garnish:**

coriander leaves

**To Serve:**

egg noodles

**Serves 4**

**Preparation time:** 5 minutes

**Cooking time:** about 12 minutes

# borlotti bean goulash

1 Heat the oil in a large flameproof casserole and fry the onion, carrots and caraway seeds for 5 minutes. Add the peppers, sweet potato, paprika and cayenne and fry for a further 3 minutes.

2 Stir in the stock, tomato purée and borlotti beans. Bring to the boil, cover and cook over a low heat for 30 minutes.

3 Meanwhile, make the dumplings. Sift the flour and salt into a bowl and stir in the suet, cheese, celery salt and a little pepper. Working quickly and lightly, gradually mix in 4–5 tablespoons of cold water – just enough to form a firm dough. Shape into 12 small balls.

4 Add the dumplings to the goulash. Cover and cook over a gentle heat for a further 20 minutes until the vegetables are tender and the dumplings are light and fluffy.

2 tablespoons extra virgin olive oil

1 onion, chopped

2 carrots, sliced

1 teaspoon caraway seeds

2 red peppers, cored, deseeded and diced

250 g (8 oz) sweet potato, diced

2 tablespoons paprika

1 teaspoon cayenne pepper

600 ml (1 pint) Vegetable Stock

2 tablespoons tomato purée

1 x 425 g (14 oz) can borlotti beans, drained

**Dumplings:**

75 g (3 oz) self-raising flour

½ teaspoon salt

50 g (2 oz) vegetarian suet

15 g (½ oz) vegetarian Cheddar cheese, grated

½ teaspoon celery salt

pepper

**Serves 4**

**Preparation time:** 25 minutes

**Cooking time:** 55–60 minutes

# bean & mushroom salad

1 In a large salad bowl, mix together the butter beans, red kidney and flageolet beans, sweetcorn, mushrooms and spring onions, reserving a tablespoon of spring onions for the garnish.

2 Put all the dressing ingredients into a screw-top jar and shake vigorously. Pour over the salad and toss well. Sprinkle the reserved spring onions over the top.

1 x 440 g (14½ oz) can butter beans, drained

1 x 440 g (14½ oz) can red kidney beans, drained

1 x 400 g (13 oz) can flageolet beans, drained

1 x 375 g (12 oz) can sweetcorn kernels, drained

125 g (4 oz) button mushrooms, quartered

1 bunch spring onions, finely chopped

**Dressing:**

4 tablespoons olive oil

1–2 tablespoons wine vinegar

¼ teaspoon mustard powder

1 garlic clove, finely chopped

salt and pepper

**Serves 8–10**

**Preparation time:** 10–15 minute

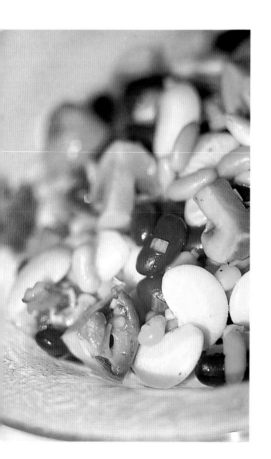

# braised vegetables with mozzarella & tomato

1 Heat the oil and butter or margarine in a large, shallow pan and gently fry the shallot over a low heat until softened.

2 Add the courgettes and cook for a few minutes over a high heat, then reduce it to medium.

3 Add the tomatoes, mash with a fork, season with salt and pepper and cook until the courgettes are tender, adding a little stock if necessary.

4 Add the olives, oregano and parsley and scatter the mozzarella over the top. Cover the pan, turn off the heat and leave the mixture to stand for a few minutes before serving.

2 tablespoons olive oil

25 g (1 oz) butter or vegetarian margarine

1 shallot, chopped

6 courgettes, cut into 5 cm (2 inch) sticks

1 x 375 g (12 oz) can plum tomatoes

2 tablespoons vegetable stock

20 black olives, halved and pitted

¼ teaspoon chopped oregano

1 tablespoon chopped parsley

1 mozzarella cheese, cubed

salt and pepper

**Serves 4**

**Preparation time:** 20 minutes

**Cooking time:** 20 minutes

roast vegetable salad •

pomelo salad •

crunchy fruit & nut salad •

country salad with horseradish dressing •

stir-fried bok choy •

hot & sour noodle & vegetable salad •

lemon & wild rice salad with papaya •

spicy aubergines with tomatoes •

polenta & vegetable terrine with roasted tomatoes •

courgettes with orange •

asparagus with balsamic & tomato dressing •

# salads & side dishes

500 g (1 lb) aubergines

4 tablespoons olive oil

4 red peppers, halved, cored and deseeded

6 garlic cloves, unpeeled

6 tomatoes

1 red chilli, deseeded and finely chopped

½ teaspoon caraway seeds

2 tablespoons lemon juice

50 g (2 oz) black olives, pitted

salt

**To Garnish:**

2 tablespoons chopped mint

| Serves 6 |
| --- |
| **Preparation time:** 15 minutes |
| **Cooking time:** 50–65 minutes |

1 Place the aubergines in a roasting tin, sprinkle with 2 tablespoons of the oil and roast in a preheated oven, 220°C (425°F) Gas Mark 7, for 20 minutes.

2 Add the peppers, garlic and tomatoes and the remaining oil. Return to the oven for 20 minutes. Remove the vegetables from the oven and leave them until they are cool enough to handle.

3 Peel and coarsely chop the aubergines, and peel and slice the peppers. Leave the garlic whole (the roasted cloves are delicious mashed with the juices when you eat the salad). Put the vegetables back in the roasting tin, stir in the chilli, caraway seeds, lemon juice and olives. Season with a little salt then cook, uncovered, for 10–15 minutes until the liquid has evaporated.

4 Remove the salad from the oven and leave to cool. Transfer the salad to a serving dish and scatter with the mint. Serve at room temperature.

If possible, make the salad a day in advance and keep it, covered, in a cool place, but not in the refrigerator.

# roast vegetable salad

# pomelo salad

1 For this very easy salad, simply place all the ingredients in a bowl and mix together thoroughly.

½ pomelo or 1 grapefruit, peeled, segmented, membranes removed and segments halved

4 shallots, sliced

½ teaspoon crushed dried chillies

2 tablespoons sugar

2 tablespoons vegetarian fish sauce or soy sauce

juice of 2 limes

¼ teaspoon salt

**Serves 2**

**Preparation time:** 8 minutes

■ A pomelo is a green-skinned, pear-shaped citrus fruit larger than a grapefruit. Its flavour is similar to grapefruit, but the flesh is not quite so juicy.

2 green-skinned dessert apples

2 red-skinned dessert apples

2 Conference pears

2 tablespoons lemon juice

1 head of celery, trimmed and sliced

50–75 g (2–3 oz) shelled walnuts

4 spring onions, trimmed and thinly sliced

**Dressing:**

1 tablespoon white wine vinegar

3 tablespoons extra virgin olive oil

2 tablespoons single cream

salt and pepper

**Serves 8**

**Preparation time:** 20 minutes

1 Core the apples and slice thinly. Place in a large bowl. Peel, core and slice the pears and add to the bowl with the lemon juice. Stir lightly but thoroughly to mix, to prevent the fruit from discolouring, then pour off the excess lemon juice. Add the celery, walnuts and spring onions.

2 To make the dressing, vigorously whisk together the vinegar and oil and season with salt and pepper. Whisk in the cream and pour the dressing over the salad. Toss lightly but thoroughly, then turn into a salad bowl, cover closely, and chill in the refrigerator until required.

# crunchy fruit & nut salad

# country salad with horseradish dressing

1 Blanch the broad beans in boiling, lightlysalted water for 1 minute, drain, refresh under cold water and pat dry on kitchen paper. Peel and discard the tough outer skin. Blanch the green beans for 1 minute, drain, refresh under cold water and pat dry on kitchen paper.

2 Place the beans in a large bowl and add the tomatoes, cucumber, celery, beetroot, onion and capers.

3 Whisk all the dressing ingredients together and season to taste. Pour the dressing over the salad and toss gently until all the ingredients are evenly coated with the dressing. Transfer the salad to a serving dish and top with the egg halves. Serve at once.

250 g (8 oz) shelled broad beans

125 g (4 oz) green beans, halved

500 g (1 lb) firm ripe plum tomatoes, cut into wedges

½ small cucumber, thinly sliced

2 celery sticks, sliced

175 g (6 oz) cooked beetroot, sliced

1 small red onion, thinly sliced

2 tablespoons drained capers

2 soft, hard-boiled eggs (see below), peeled and halved

**Dressing:**

2 tablespoons grated horseradish or 1 tablespoon creamed horseradish

4 tablespoons extra virgin olive oil

2 teaspoons red wine vinegar

pinch of sugar

2 tablespoons chopped herbs

salt and pepper

| Serves 4 |
| --- |
| **Preparation time:** 20 minutes |
| **Cooking time:** 10 minutes |

■ When hard-boiling the eggs, carefully spoon them into a pan of simmering water. Return to the boil and cook for 8 minutes. Drain and plunge into cold water. Peel and halve when required.

vegetarian

# stir-fried bok-choy

1 Trim the white stalks of the bok-choy, then cut the stalks into 4 cm (1½ inch) lengths. Tear or coarsely shred the green leaves.

2 Heat an empty wok until hot. Add the groundnut oil and heat until hot. Add the bok-choy stalks, garlic, sugar and a pinch of salt. Crumble the dried chillies over the bok-choy and stir-fry over a moderate to high heat for 2 minutes.

3 Add the bok-choy leaves, soy sauce and vinegar and toss vigorously for 30–60 seconds until the leaves start to wilt. Serve immediately, sprinkled with sesame oil.

■ Bok-choy, which you may also see labelled as bok-choi and pak-choi, can be bought in Chinese supermarkets and green-grocers. It is a good-looking vegetable, with pure white crunchy stalks and contrasting dark green leaves. Its flavour is pleasantly bitter.

375 g (12 oz) bok-choy

2 tablespoons groundnut oil

2 garlic cloves, finely chopped

2 teaspoons sugar

2 dried red chillies

1 tablespoon soy sauce

1 tablespoon rice wine vinegar or white wine or cider vinegar

salt

sesame oil, to finish

**Serves 3–4**

**Preparation time:** 10 minutes

**Cooking time:** about 5 minutes

½ cucumber, peeled, halved and deseeded

50 g (2 oz) vermicelli rice noodles

1 carrot, cut into long julienne strips

1 red chilli, deseeded and cut into long julienne strips

2 tablespoons chopped coriander

salt

**Dressing:**

2 tablespoons sunflower oil

½ teaspoon sesame oil

2 teaspoons caster sugar

2 tablespoons lime juice

1 tablespoon vegetarian fish sauce or soy sauce

salt and pepper

**To Garnish:**

coriander sprigs

1 Sprinkle the cucumber with a little salt and set aside to drain for 30 minutes. Put the noodles in a bowl, cover with boiling water and soak for 4–6 minutes, or according to the packet instructions. Wash and dry the cucumber. Thoroughly drain the noodles and put them in a large bowl.

2 Combine all the dressing ingredients together and season with salt and pepper to taste. Add half to the noodles and toss well.

3 Cut the cucumber into long thin julienne strips and add to the noodles together with the julienne strips of carrot and chilli. Stir in the coriander and the remaining dressing and serve at once, garnished with coriander sprigs.

**Serves 4–6**

**Preparation time:** 15 minutes, plus draining and soaking

# hot & sour noodle & vegetable salad

# lemon & wild rice salad with papaya

1 Cook the wild rice in plenty of lightly salted, boiling water for 35 minutes until tender.

2 Meanwhile, put the long-grain rice in a pan with plenty of cold water, add the lemon juice, sugar and salt, bring to the boil and simmer gently for 10–12 minutes until cooked.

3 Drain both the wild and long-grain rice and place in a large bowl. Blend all the dressing ingredients together, season and toss with the rice. Set aside until cold.

4 Just before serving, cut the papaya in half, discard the seeds and peel and dice the flesh. Add to the rice with the spring onions, nuts and seeds. Taste and adjust the seasoning, if necessary, and serve at once.

50 g (2 oz) wild rice, rinsed

250 g (8 oz) long-grain rice, rinsed

2 tablespoons lemon juice

1 teaspoon sugar

1 teaspoon salt

1 small papaya

1 bunch spring onions, sliced

25 g (1 oz) pecan nuts, toasted and chopped

25 g (1 oz) Brazil nuts, toasted and chopped

25 g (1 oz) sunflower seeds, toasted

1 tablespoon poppy seeds

**Dressing:**

6 tablespoons extra virgin olive oil

1 tablespoon lemon juice or lime juice

2 tablespoons chopped parsley

salt and pepper

**Serves 6**

**Preparation time:** 15 minutes

**Cooking time:** 35 minutes

# spicy aubergines with tomatoes

1   Place the aubergines in a bowl and stir in the lemon juice.

2   Melt the ghee in a large pre-heated wok and gently fry the onions, garlic and ginger for 4–5 minutes until soft. Add the black onion seeds, cinnamon, coriander and cumin seeds and stir well. Fry the mixture for a further 2 minutes, then stir in the pepper, salt, garam masala, turmeric and chilli powder.

3   Add the tomatoes with their juices and the tomato purée, stir well and bring to the boil. Pour in the boiling water and stir in the aubergine pieces with the lemon juice. Bring to the boil, lower the heat and simmer gently for 15–20 minutes until soft. Garnish with the dried red chillies and serve hot.

▦ Garam masala is a mixture of spices. There is no set recipe, and most Indian cooks prepare it according to their own taste. Ready-made garam masala is available from supermarkets and Indian food stores.

750 g (1½ lb) aubergines, cut into 4 cm (1½ inch) chunks

juice of 1 lemon

175 g (6 oz) vegetable ghee

2 onions, thinly sliced

4 garlic cloves, thinly sliced

7.5 cm (3 inch) piece of fresh root ginger, peeled and thinly sliced

2 teaspoons black onion seeds

7.5 cm (3 inch) piece of cinnamon stick

2 teaspoons coriander seeds

2 teaspoons cumin seeds

2 teaspoons pepper

2 teaspoons salt

2 teaspoons garam masala

1½ teaspoons ground turmeric

1 teaspoon chilli powder

1 x 400 g (13 oz) can chopped tomatoes

125 g (4 oz) tomato purée

600 ml (1 pint) boiling water

**To Garnish:**

dried red chillies

**Serves 4–6**

**Preparation time:** 15 minutes

**Cooking time:** 25–30 minutes

# polenta & vegetable terrine with roasted tomatoes

1 Brush a 1.25 kg (2½ lb) loaf tin with olive oil. Put the red pepper under a preheated grill for 10 minutes until blistered. Seal in a polythene bag and set aside to cool. Peel off the charred skin and remove the seeds. Cut the flesh into 2.5 cm (1 inch) strips.

2 Heat half the oil in a frying pan, add the mushrooms and onions, cover and cook for 2–3 minutes. Remove with a slotted spoon and drain on kitchen paper. Blanch the remaining vegetables in separate saucepans of boiling salted water until just tender. Drain, refresh under cold running water and drain again.

3 Bring the measured water to the boil in a large saucepan. Add a pinch of salt, then pour in the polenta, stirring constantly for about 20 minutes until the mixture leaves the sides of the pan. Remove from the heat, add the vegetables and Parmesan, mix well and spoon into the loaf tin. Level the surface and set aside until cold. Turn the terrine out of the tin and cut it into slices. Brush each side with a little of the oil.

4 Mix the garlic with the remaining oil, brush it over the tomatoes and season to taste. Place the terrine slices and tomatoes, cut side down, under a preheated moderate grill for 6–8 minutes, turning once. Serve the terrine topped with the tomato halves, garnished with the olives and sprinkled with Parmesan.

4 tablespoons olive oil, plus extra for brushing

1 red pepper

250 g (8 oz) mushrooms, quartered

2 red onions, cut into small wedges

125 g (4 oz) baby courgettes, cut in half lengthways

125 g (4 oz) baby carrots

125 g (4 oz) French beans, topped and tailed

125 g (4 oz) broccoli, cut into florets

1.5 litres (2½ pints) water

300 g (10 oz) polenta

50 g (2 oz) vegetarian Parmesan cheese, grated, plus extra for sprinkling

2 garlic cloves, crushed

8 ripe plum tomatoes, cut in half lengthways

50 g (2 oz) black olives, to garnish

salt and pepper

**Serves 6–8**

**Preparation time:** 1 hour 10 minutes

**Cooking time:** 6–8 minutes

■ Polenta is fine golden cornmeal which comes originally from Italy. It is widely available from supermarkets.

# courgettes with orange

1 Place the courgettes and orange rind and juice together in a saucepan. Cover tightly and simmer for about 6 minutes or until the courgettes are just tender.

2 Add the butter or margarine and then season with pepper to taste. Allow the butter or margarine to melt slightly, then toss carefully until the courgettes are well coated. Serve at once.

750 g (1½ lb) courgettes, sliced

grated rind and juice of 2 oranges

25 g (1 oz) butter or vegetarian margarine

pepper

**Serves 6**

**Preparation time:** 10 minutes

**Cooking time:** about 6 minutes

500 g (1 lb) young asparagus spears, trimmed

2 tablespoons extra virgin olive oil

50 g (2 oz) pine nuts, toasted

25 g (1 oz) vegetarian Parmesan cheese shavings

sea salt and pepper

**Dressing:**

2 tablespoons balsamic vinegar

1–2 garlic cloves, crushed

375 g (12 oz) tomatoes, skinned, deseeded and chopped

5 tablespoons extra virgin olive oil

**1** To make the dressing, mix the vinegar, garlic, tomatoes and olive oil in a bowl. Set aside.

**2** Brush the asparagus with olive oil and cook on an oiled barbecue grill over hot coals or under a preheated moderate grill for 5–6 minutes until tender.

**3** Divide the grilled asparagus among 4 warmed serving plates. Spoon over the balsamic and tomato dressing, top with the pine nuts and Parmesan and sprinkle with the sea salt and pepper. Serve at once.

**Serves 5**

**Preparation time:** 15 minutes

**Cooking time:** 5–6 minutes

# asparagus with balsamic & tomato dressing

crusted cassoulet ●

provençal pancakes ●

stuffed pancakes ●

spinach paneer ●

cauliflower pachadi ●

sweet potato & spinach curry ●

thai yellow curry with carrot ●

stuffed thai omelette ●

moroccan stew with couscous ●

moroccan orange & olive salad ●

roasted vegetable pizza ●

melanzane parmigiana ●

potato gnocchi with fennel sauce ●

# around the world

# crusted cassoulet

1   Drain the beans and place in a saucepan with the measured water. Bring to the boil and boil rapidly for about 10 minutes. Lower the heat, cover and simmer for 45 minutes. Drain the beans and reserve 300 ml (½ pint) of the cooking liquid.

2   Soak the dried ceps in the boiling water for 20 minutes, then drain, reserving the liquid. Slice the ceps.

3   Heat half the oil in a frying pan and fry the garlic and onions for 5 minutes. Add the mushrooms and herbs and stir-fry for a further 5 minutes until the mushrooms are golden. Remove from the pan with a slotted spoon and set aside. Heat the remaining oil in the frying pan and fry the carrots, celery and pepper for 5 minutes. Add the wine and boil rapidly for 3 minutes. Stir in the beans and their liquid, the mushroom mixture, the ceps and their liquid, the tomato purée and soy sauce and season to taste. Spoon into 4 small ovenproof dishes or 1 large gratin dish.

4   Layer the sliced bread over the cassoulet. Mix together the oil, garlic and thyme, brush over the bread and scatter with the Parmesan. Cover loosely with foil and place in a preheated oven, 190°C (375°F) Gas Mark 5, for 30 minutes. Remove the foil and bake for a further 20 minutes until the crust is golden.

125 g (4 oz) dried haricot beans, soaked overnight

1.2 litres (2 pints) water

15 g (½ oz) dried ceps

150 ml (¼ pint) boiling water

6 tablespoons extra virgin olive oil

2 garlic cloves, chopped

250 g (8 oz) baby onions, halved

175 g (6 oz) mixed mushrooms, sliced

1 tablespoon each chopped thyme, rosemary and sage

2 carrots, diced

2 celery sticks, sliced

1 red pepper, cored, deseeded and diced

150 ml (¼ pint) red wine

4 tablespoons tomato purée

1 tablespoon dark soy sauce

salt and pepper

**Topping:**

½ small French stick, thinly sliced

2 tablespoons extra virgin olive oil

1 garlic clove, crushed

2 tablespoons chopped thyme

25 g (1 oz) vegetarian Parmesan cheese, grated

**Serves 6**

**Preparation time:** 40 minutes, plus soaking

**Cooking time:** 1½–1¾ hours

# provençal pancakes

1 To make the batter, sift the buckwheat flour, plain flour and salt into a mixing bowl. Make a well in the centre and add the egg and half the milk. Beat the liquid ingredients with a wooden spoon to mix, then gradually draw in the flour, stirring well. When the mixture is smooth, stir in the remaining milk. Cover and chill for 1–2 hours.

2 Lightly oil a 15 cm (6 inch) omelette pan and set over a medium heat. Pour in about 3 tablespoons of the batter and tilt and rotate the pan to coat the base evenly, then tip out any excess batter. Cook for 30–45 seconds until the pancake is just set and the underside is golden brown. Loosen the edge with a palette knife and turn or flip the pancake over. Cook the other side for 30 seconds, then slide out of the pan. Cook the remaining pancakes in the same way.

3 To make the filling, heat the oil in a frying pan and gently fry the onion until soft. Add the garlic, aubergines and pepper and stir-fry for 10 minutes.

4 Add the tomatoes and tomato purée, cover and cook for 15 minutes. Season to taste. Fill, roll and serve the pancakes at once, sprinkled with the Parmesan.

50 g (2 oz) buckwheat flour

50 g (2 oz) plain flour

salt

1 egg, beaten

300 ml (½ pint) milk

1 tablespoon vegetable oil

grated vegetarian Parmesan cheese, to serve

**Filling:**

2 tablespoons olive oil

1 onion, chopped

2 garlic cloves, crushed

1 small aubergine, chopped

1 green or red pepper, cored, deseeded and chopped

4 large tomatoes, skinned and chopped

1 tablespoon tomato purée

salt and pepper

**Makes 12**

**Preparation time:** 15 minutes, plus chilling

**Cooking time:** 50 minutes

# stuffed pancakes

1 To make the batter, sift the flour and salt into a mixing bowl. Make a well in the centre and add the eggs and milk. Beat the liquid ingredients with a wooden spoon to mix, then gradually draw in the flour, stirring well. When the mixture is smooth, stir in the water. Cover and chill for 1–2 hours.

2 Lightly oil an 18 cm (7 inch) omelette pan and set over a medium heat. Pour in 3–4 tablespoons of the batter and tilt and rotate the pan to coat the base evenly, then tip out any excess batter. Cook for 30–45 seconds until the pancake is just set and the underside is golden brown. Loosen the edge with a palette knife and turn or flip the pancake over. Cook the other side for 30 seconds, then slide out of the pan. Cook the remaining pancakes in the same way.

3 To make the filling, chop the spinach. Stir in the egg, ricotta and Parmesan. Season to taste. Divide the filling among the pancakes, roll up and put in an ovenproof dish. Top with the butter and Parmesan and add the stock. Bake in a preheated oven, 200°C (400°F) Gas Mark 6, for 20 minutes. Serve at once.

125 g (4 oz) plain flour

¼ teaspoon salt

2 eggs

150 ml (¼ pint) milk

6 tablespoons water

1 tablespoon oil

25 g (1 oz) butter, diced

25 g (1 oz) vegetarian Parmesan cheese, grated

5 tablespoons vegetable stock

**Filling:**

250 g (8 oz) cooked spinach

1 egg, beaten

250 g (8 oz) ricotta cheese

25 g (1 oz) grated vegetarian Parmesan cheese, grated

salt and pepper

**Makes 8**

**Preparation time:** 25 minutes, plus chilling

**Cooking time:** 30 minutes

# spinach paneer

1 Cut the paneer into 2.5 cm (1 inch) cubes and set it aside. Steam the spinach for 3–4 minutes until it has wilted, leave it to cool and then place it in a food processor and process briefly to purée it. Set aside.

2 Heat the ghee in a heavy-based saucepan and fry the paneer cubes, turning occasionally, for 10 minutes or until they are golden. Remove from the pan and set aside.

3 Add the onion, garlic, chilli and ginger to the hot ghee and fry gently over a low heat, stirring constantly, for 5 minutes, until softened. Stir in the turmeric, coriander, chilli powder and cumin, and fry for 1 minute more. Stir in the fried paneer and cook, covered, for a further 5 minutes. Taste and season with salt, if necessary, and serve immediately.

250 g (8 oz) paneer

375 g (12 oz) young leaf spinach, washed and patted dry

2 tablespoons vegetable ghee

1 large onion, chopped

2 garlic cloves, crushed

1 large green chilli, deseeded and sliced

1 tablespoon grated fresh root ginger

1 teaspoon ground turmeric

1 teaspoon ground coriander

1 teaspoon chilli powder

½ teaspoon ground cumin

salt

**Serves 4**

**Preparation time: 15 minutes**

**Cooking time: 30 minutes**

■ Paneer is Indian curd cheese and it is available from good Indian grocers. Once the main fat used in India, ghee is clarified butter, but vegetable ghee is now more popular as it is lower in fat. Both are available from supermarkets and Indian food stores.

# cauliflower pachadi

1 Place the cauliflower florets in a bowl with the buttermilk, salt and some pepper and mix well. Set aside for 2 hours to marinate.

2 Heat the ghee in a heavy-based saucepan and fry the onion, garlic and ginger over a gentle heat, stirring occasionally, for about 8 minutes until softened and light golden. Add the 2 types of mustard seeds, turmeric and desiccated coconut and cook for a further 3 minutes, stirring constantly.

3 Stir in the cauliflower with the buttermilk marinade and 150 ml (¼ pint) water. Bring the curry to the boil, then reduce the heat, cover and simmer gently for 12 minutes or until the cauliflower is tender.

4 Remove the lid, taste and adjust the seasoning, if necessary, and stir in the coriander. Increase the heat and cook the cauliflower pachadi for a further 3–4 minutes to thicken the sauce. Serve hot with steamed rice or naan bread.

375 g (2 oz) cauliflower florets

150 ml (¼ pint) buttermilk

1 teaspoon salt

3 tablespoons vegetable ghee

1 large onion, finely sliced

2 garlic cloves, crushed

1 tablespoon freshly grated root ginger

1 teaspoon mustard seeds

1 teaspoon black mustard seeds

1 teaspoon ground turmeric

25 g (1 oz) desiccated coconut

2 tablespoons chopped coriander

pepper

**To Serve:**

steamed rice or naan bread

**Serves 4**

**Preparation time:** 10 minutes, plus marinating

**Cooking time:** 30 minutes

# sweet potato & spinach curry

1 Cook the sweet potato chunks in a pan of salted boiling water for 8–10 minutes or until tender. Drain and set aside.

2 Heat the oil in a saucepan and fry the onion, garlic and turmeric over a gentle heat, stirring frequently, for 3 minutes. Stir in the chilli and fry for a further 2 minutes.

3 Add the coconut milk, stir to mix and simmer for 3–4 minutes until the coconut milk has thickened slightly. Stir in the sweet potatoes and salt to taste and cook the curry for 4 minutes.

4 Stir in the spinach, cover the pan and simmer gently for 2–3 minutes or until the spinach has wilted and the curry has heated through. Taste, adjust the seasoning if necessary and serve immediately.

500 g (1 lb) sweet potato, peeled and cut into large chunks

3 tablespoons groundnut oil

1 red onion, chopped

2 garlic cloves, crushed

1 teaspoon ground turmeric

1 large red chilli, deseeded and chopped

400 ml (14 fl oz) coconut milk

250 g (8 oz) young leaf spinach

salt

**Serves 4**

**Preparation time:** 10 minutes

**Cooking time:** 25 minutes

# thai yellow curry with carrot

1 Put the stock in a saucepan, add 5 of the lime leaves, the galangal or ginger, carrots, chillies and half the garlic. Simmer for 15 minutes. Strain the stock, reserving the liquid and both the carrots and chillies separately.

2 Heat the oil in a saucepan and fry the remaining garlic for 1 minute. Add the reserved carrot and the peanuts and cook, stirring, for 1 minute. Add the coconut milk and curry paste and stir until well blended. Add the reserved liquid, the mushrooms and shallots and simmer, stirring occasionally, for 15 minutes or until the shallots are cooked. Season with salt to taste.

3 Seed and finely slice the reserved chillies. Use as a garnish for the curry, together with the remaining lime leaves.

150 ml (¼ pint) vegetable stock

8 lime leaves

25 g (1 oz) galangal, peeled and sliced or fresh root ginger

175 g (6 oz) carrots, cut into chunks

2 large red and green chillies

4 garlic cloves, crushed

1 tablespoon groundnut oil

2 tablespoons crushed roasted peanuts

300 ml (½ pint) coconut milk

2 tablespoons yellow curry paste

8 canned straw mushrooms, drained

4 shallots

salt

**Serves 2**

**Preparation time:** 15 minutes

**Cooking time:** 35–40 minutes

■ Galangal is a member of the ginger family and is used in South-east Asian cooking. Fresh root ginger may be used instead.

1 First make the filling: heat the oil in a preheated wok and stir-fry the garlic and onion for 30 seconds. Add the beans, asparagus, corn cobs, tomato, mushrooms, sugar and soy sauce and stir-fry for 3–4 minutes, then add the water and a pinch of salt and continue stir-frying for 2 minutes. Remove the filling from the wok and set aside. Wipe the wok clean with kitchen paper.

2 Make the omelette: Heat the oil in a preheated wok, swirling it round to coat the base and sides. Pour off any excess. Pour in the eggs, swirling them around in the wok to form a large, thin omelette. Loosen the omelette and move it around with a spatula to stop it sticking, adding a little more oil if necessary.

3 When the omelette is almost firm, spoon the filling into the middle and fold both sides and ends over to form an oblong parcel, constantly checking that the omelette is not sticking underneath.

4 Carefully remove the omelette from the wok and place in a serving dish. Serve the cooked dish at once garnished with crispy basil.

1 tablespoon groundnut oil

3 eggs, beaten

salt and pepper

**Filling:**

3 tablespoons groundnut oil

2 garlic cloves, chopped

1 onion, finely chopped

2 tablespoons chopped French beans

2 tablespoons chopped asparagus

3 baby corn cobs, thinly sliced

1 tomato, diced

4 dried shiitake mushrooms, soaked, drained and sliced

1½ teaspoons sugar

2 teaspoons soy sauce

50 ml (2 fl oz) water

salt

**To Garnish:**

Crispy Basil (see page 9)

**Serves 2**

**Preparation time:** 8–10 minutes, plus soaking

**Cooking time:** 8–10 minutes

# stuffed thai omelette

# moroccan stew with couscous

1 Put the lentils in a saucepan with the water. Bring to the boil, cover and simmer for 20 minutes. Meanwhile, heat half the oil in a large saucepan and fry the onions, garlic and spices for 5 minutes. Add the potatoes and carrots and fry for a further 5 minutes. Add the lentils with their cooking liquid, cover and simmer gently for 15 minutes.

2 Rinse the couscous several times under cold running water to moisten all the grains, then spread out on a large baking sheet. Sprinkle with a little water and then leave to soak for 15 minutes.

3 Heat the remaining oil in a frying pan and fry the courgettes and mushrooms for 4–5 minutes until lightly golden. Add to the lentil mixture with the tomato juice, tomato purée, dried apricots and chilli sauce and return to the boil. Cook for a further 10 minutes until the vegetables and lentils are tender.

4 Steam the couscous according to the packet instructions or over the stew in a double boiler for 6–7 minutes. Transfer to a large warmed bowl, spoon the vegetable and lentil stew over the top and serve the juices separately, with extra chilli sauce if liked.

125 g (4 oz) green lentils, rinsed

600 ml (1 pint) water

4 tablespoons extra virgin olive oil

2 small onions, cut into wedges

2 garlic cloves, chopped

1 tablespoon ground coriander

2 teaspoons ground cumin

1 teaspoon ground turmeric

1 teaspoon ground cinnamon

12 new potatoes, halved if large

2 large carrots, thickly sliced

250 g (8 oz) couscous

2 courgettes, sliced

175 g (6 oz) button mushrooms

300 ml (½ pint) tomato juice

1 tablespoon tomato purée

125 g (4 oz) ready-to-eat dried apricots, chopped

2 tablespoons chilli sauce, plus extra to serve (optional)

**Serves 4–6**

**Preparation time:** 40–45 minutes, plus soaking

**Cooking time:** 40 minutes

# moroccan orange & olive salad

1 Heat a small heavy-based frying pan and dry-fry the cumin seeds until fragrant. Tip into a grinder and grind to a powder.

2 Remove the rind from 1 of the oranges with a zester and set aside. Peel the oranges with a sharp knife, carefully removing all the pith. Working over a bowl to catch the juice, cut out the segments from the oranges and discard any pips. Put the oranges and olives into the bowl.

3 Whisk or shake together the oil, harissa and roasted cumin. Add salt to taste, then pour the dressing over the oranges and olives and toss the salad together.

4 Arrange the lettuce leaves on 4 plates. Add the orange and olive mixture. Garnish with the reserved orange rind and dill sprigs and serve.

■ Made from peppers, olive oil, garlic, coriander, cayenne pepper, cumin and mint, harissa is a North African purée used as a condiment. It is available from most supermarkets.

2 teaspoons cumin seeds

4 large oranges

125 g (4 oz) green olives

50 ml (2 fl oz) extra virgin olive oil

1 tablespoon harissa, or to taste

1 crisp lettuce, torn into bite-size pieces

salt

dill sprigs, to garnish

**Serves 4**

**Preparation time**: 15 minutes

**Cooking time**: 1 minute

# roasted vegetable pizza

1 First make the dough. Sift the flour, yeast and salt into a bowl. Make a well in the centre and add the sun-dried tomatoes and oil. Gradually pour in the water, stir vigorously, drawing in the flour a little at a time to form a soft dough. Knead the dough for at least 10 minutes until it feels smooth and springy. Place the dough in an oiled bowl, turning once so that the surface is coated. Cover the bowl with a cloth and leave to rise in a warm place for 1–2 hours until doubled in size.

2 Meanwhile, make the tomato sauce. Put all the ingredients in a pan and bring to the boil. Simmer briskly, uncovered, for 20–25 minutes, until the sauce is very thick.

3 When the dough has risen sufficiently, knock it back and turn it out on to a floured surface. Knead again briefly for 2–3 minutes. Roll the dough out to a 30 cm (12 inch) circle and place on a greased baking sheet.

4 Mix all the vegetables together in a roasting tin, add the garlic, oil and rosemary and season with salt and pepper. Turn the mixture over several times to coat the vegetables evenly. Roast in a preheated oven, 200°C (400°F) Gas Mark 6, for 35 minutes until the vegetables are tender.

5 Spread the tomato sauce evenly over the dough. Arrange the roasted vegetables on the top and sprinkle with Parmesan. Season with salt and pepper. Bake the pizza in the preheated oven for 20 minutes. Serve immediately.

**Sun-Dried Tomato Dough:**

250 g (8 oz) unbleached strong plain flour

1 teaspoon easy-blend dried yeast

1 teaspoon salt

25 g (1 oz) sun-dried tomatoes in oil, drained (reserve 1 tablespoon) and finely chopped

125–150 ml (4 fl oz–¼ pint) warm water

**Tomato Sauce:**

3 tablespoons olive oil

1 x 425 g (14 oz) can chopped tomatoes

1 teaspoon dried oregano

pinch of sugar

salt and pepper

**Topping:**

1 aubergine, sliced

1 yellow pepper, cored, deseeded and cut into strips

1 red onion, cut into small wedges

1 courgette, cut into sticks

3 garlic cloves, thickly sliced

3 tablespoons olive oil

2 teaspoons chopped rosemary

2 tablespoons vegetarian Parmesan cheese, grated

salt and pepper

**Makes** 1 x 30 cm (12 inch) pizza

**Preparation time:** 20 minutes, plus rising

**Cooking time:** 55 minutes

# melanzane parmigiana

1 Cut the aubergines lengthways into thick slices. Sprinkle with salt and leave to drain in a colander for 30 minutes. Wash well, drain and pat dry on kitchen paper.

2 Brush the aubergine slices with oil and place them on 2 large baking sheets. Roast the aubergines at the top of a preheated oven, 200°C (400°F) Gas Mark 6, for 10 minutes on each side until they are golden and tender. Meanwhile, reheat the tomato sauce and keep warm.

3 Spoon a little of the tomato sauce into an ovenproof dish and top with a layer of aubergines and some of the Cheddar. Continue with the layers, finishing with the Cheddar. Sprinkle with the Parmesan cheese and bake for 30 minutes until the cheese is bubbling and golden.

6 aubergines

salt

2 tablespoons extra virgin olive oil

1 quantity Tomato Sauce (see page 74)

250 g (8 oz) vegetarian Cheddar cheese, grated

50 g (2 oz) vegetarian Parmesan cheese, grated

**Serves 6**

**Preparation time:** 10 minutes, plus draining, plus making sauce

**Cooking time:** 50 minutes

# potato gnocchi with fennel sauce

1 Bake the potatoes in a preheated oven, 200°C (400°F) Gas Mark 6, for 1 hour or until tender. Wearing a pair of rubber gloves, peel the potatoes while hot. Lightly mash the potato and beat in the egg, egg yolk and just enough of the flour to form a soft, slightly sticky dough.

2 Brush an ovenproof dish with oil. Bring a large saucepan of lightly salted water to a rolling boil. Roll small pieces of the potato dough in your hands and drop them into the boiling water. Cook in batches for 4–5 minutes until they rise to the surface. With a slotted spoon, drain and place in the prepared dish. Repeat with the remaining mixture.

3 Whisk all the sauce ingredients together, season and pour over the gnocchi. Heat through in the oven for 6–8 minutes until bubbling. Serve at once sprinkled with grated Parmesan and garnished with fennel fronds.

1 kg ( 2 lb) floury potatoes

1 egg

1 egg yolk

175 g (6 oz) plain flour

oil, for brushing

salt

freshly grated vegetarian Parmesan cheese, to serve

**Fennel Sauce:**

4 tablespoons extra virgin olive oil

2 tablespoons boiling water

1 tablespoon lemon juice

2 tablespoons chopped fennel fronds

salt and pepper

a few fennel fronds, to garnish

**Serves 4**

**Preparation time:** 50 minutes

**Cooking time:** 1¼ hours

filo horns with mixed berries & raspberry sauce ●

blackcurrant sorbet ●

pineapple & mango clafoutis ●

peach, apricot & blueberry gratin ●

boston brownies ●

pear & cardamom flan ●

rhubarb, apple & double ginger crumble ●

rum pancakes ●

chilled fig soup ●

orange tart ●

double orange slices ●

lemon soufflé pancakes ●

fresh lemon slices ●

# desserts to die for

1 Grease 6 cream horn moulds. Cut each sheet of pastry into 2 x 15 cm (6 inch) squares, brush each square with butter or margarine and fold in half diagonally to form 12 triangles. Wrap 1 triangle around each mould, brush with the remaining butter or margarine and place on a large greased baking sheet, seam-side down. Bake the filo horns in a pre-heated oven, 190°C (375°F) Gas Mark 5, for 15 minutes until crisp and golden. Leave to cool before carefully extracting the pastry from the moulds.

2 Beat together the ricotta or curd cheese, honey and almonds. Hull and slice the berries as necessary.

3 To make the sauce, place the raspberries in a blender or food processor and process until smooth. Pass through a fine sieve to remove the pips. Alternatively, rub the whole raspberries through a fine sieve. Whisk in the Grand Marnier, if using, and the icing sugar.

4 Just before serving, pipe the ricotta mixture into the filo horns to come two-thirds of the way to the top. Pile in the berries and serve 2 horns per person with the raspberry sauce. Dust with sifted icing sugar and scatter with toasted flaked almonds.

75 g (3 oz) unsalted butter or vegetarian margarine, melted, plus extra for greasing

6 large sheets filo pastry, thawed if frozen

175 g (6 oz) ricotta or curd cheese

1 tablespoon clear honey

25 g (1 oz) ground almonds, toasted

625 g (1¼ lb) mixed summer berries

**Sauce:**

250 g (8 oz) frozen raspberries, thawed

2 tablespoons Grand Marnier (optional)

3 tablespoons icing sugar, plus extra for dusting

toasted flaked almonds, to decorate

**Serves 6**

**Preparation time:** 40 minutes

**Cooking time:** 15 minutes

# filo horns with mixed berries & raspberry sauce

# blackcurrant sorbet

1 Place the blackcurrants in a saucepan with 2 tablespoons of the water and simmer until tender. Rub through a sieve: there should be 300 ml (½ pint) blackcurrant purée.

2 Place the sugar and the remaining water in a saucepan and heat gently, stirring constantly, until dissolved. Bring to the boil and simmer for 5 minutes. Leave to cool.

3 Add the sugar syrup to the blackcurrant purée with the lemon juice. Turn the purée into a rigid freezerproof container. Cover and freeze until partially set.

4 When the sorbet is half frozen, fold in the egg white. Freeze until firm. Transfer the sorbet to the refrigerator 10 minutes before serving to soften a little. Serve on chilled plates, garnished with mint.

500 g (1 lb) blackcurrants

150 ml (¼ pint) water

125 g (4 oz) caster sugar

2 tablespoons lemon juice

1 egg white, lightly whisked

mint leaves, to garnish

---

**Serves 4**

**Preparation time:** 15 minutes, plus freezing

**Cooking time:** 15 minutes

# pineapple & mango clafoutis

1 Cut the pineapple and mango flesh into 1 cm (½ inch) chunks. Put the prepared fruit in a bowl and sprinkle with the rum. Set aside while you make the batter.

2 Break the eggs into a bowl and beat lightly together. Sift the flour and salt and blend well with the beaten eggs. Whisk in the sugar until the mixture is smooth.

3 Heat the milk with the vanilla pod but do not allow it to boil. Remove from the heat and set aside to infuse for 5 minutes. Remove the vanilla pod and strain the milk into the egg mixture, a little at a time, beating well until thoroughly blended. Beat in the rum from the soaked fruit.

4 Arrange the pineapple and mango in a greased shallow, ovenproof dish. Pour the batter mixture over them and bake in a pre-heated oven, 200°C (400°F) Gas Mark 6, for 25–30 minutes until risen and set. Cool a little and serve lukewarm, sprinkled with caster sugar.

500 g (1 lb) pineapple and mango, peeled

2 tablespoons dark rum

3 eggs

20 g (¾ oz) plain flour

pinch of salt

50 g (2 oz) caster sugar

300 ml (½ pint) milk

1 vanilla pod

butter or vegetarian margarine, for greasing

caster sugar, for sprinkling

**Serves 4–6**

**Preparation time:** 15 minutes

**Cooking time:** 25–30 minutes

4 firm ripe peaches, halved, stoned and very thinly sliced

6 firm ripe apricots, halved, stoned and very thinly sliced

175 g (6 oz) blueberries

250 g (8 oz) mascarpone cheese

250 ml (8 fl oz) Greek yogurt

3 tablespoons light muscovado sugar

1 teaspoon ground cinnamon

**Serves 6**

**Preparation time:** 10 minutes

**Cooking time:** 5–6 minutes

1 Spoon the peaches, apricots and blueberries into a gratin dish.

2 Beat the mascarpone and yogurt together and spread the mixture evenly over the fruit.

3 Combine the sugar and cinnamon, sprinkle over the gratin to cover the surface and cook under a preheated hot grill for 5–6 minutes until the sugar is caramelized. Leave to cool for a few minutes before serving.

# peach, apricot & blueberry gratin

# boston brownies

1 Grease and line a 30 x 20 x 5 cm (12 x 8 x 2 inch) baking tin.

2 Beat the butter or margarine with the soft light brown sugar until light. Gradually beat in the eggs and vanilla. Sift the flour, baking powder, salt and cocoa powder over the mixture and fold in. Stir in the toasted hazelnuts, chopped chocolate and mini marshmallows.

3 Spoon the mixture into the prepared tin and bake in a preheated oven, 180°C (350°F) Gas Mark 4, for 30–35 minutes. Leave in the tin to cool, before cutting into 12 pieces.

250 g (8 oz) butter or vegetarian margarine, softened, plus extra for greasing

250 g (8 oz) soft light brown sugar

4 eggs, beaten

1 teaspoon vanilla extract

200 g (7 oz) plain flour

1 teaspoon baking powder

½ teaspoon salt

50 g (2 oz) cocoa powder

125 g (4 oz) toasted hazelnuts, chopped

125 g (4 oz) plain chocolate, chopped

125 g (4 oz) mini marshmallows

**Makes 12**

**Preparation time:** 15 minutes

**Cooking time:** 30–35 minutes

# pear & cardamom flan

1 Sift the flour and salt into a bowl and rub in the butter or margarine until the mixture resembles fine breadcrumbs. Stir in the sugar and slowly work in the egg yolk and water to form a soft dough. Knead lightly, wrap in foil and chill for 30 minutes. Roll out the pastry on a lightly floured surface and use to line a greased 23 cm (9 inch) fluted flan tin. Prick the base and chill for a further 20 minutes.

2 Line the pastry case with non-stick baking paper and baking beans. Place in a preheated oven, 220°C (425°F) Gas Mark 7, for 10 minutes. Remove the paper and beans and bake for a further 10–12 minutes until the pastry is crisp and golden. Remove from the oven and reduce the temperature to 180°C (350°F) Gas Mark 4.

3 Make the filling. Beat together the butter or margarine and sugar until pale and light and then beat in the eggs, until incorporated. Lightly beat in all the remaining ingredients, except the pears. Pour the mixture into the prepared pastry case.

4 Peel and halve the pears and scoop out the cores. Thinly slice each pear lengthways. Be careful not to change the shape of the pears. Then, using a palette knife, carefully transfer the sliced pears to the pastry case, arranging them neatly on the filling. Bake the flan for 55–60 minutes until golden and firm in the middle. Serve the flan warm, sprinkled all over with a little caster sugar and some whipped cream, if liked.

175 g (6 oz) plain flour

¼ teaspoon salt

100 g (3½ oz) unsalted butter or vegetarian margarine, diced, plus extra for greasing

2 tablespoons caster sugar

1 egg yolk

1–2 tablespoons cold water

**Filling:**

125 g (4 oz) unsalted butter or vegetarian margarine, softened

75 g (3 oz) caster sugar

2 small eggs, lightly beaten

75 g (3 oz) ground hazelnuts

25 g (1 oz) ground rice

seeds from 2 cardamom pods, crushed

1 teaspoon grated lemon rind

4 tablespoons soured cream

3 small firm pears

**To Serve:**

1 teaspoon caster sugar (optional)

whipped cream (optional)

**Serves 6**

**Preparation time:** 20 minutes, plus chilling

**Cooking time:** 1 hour 20 minutes

125 g (4 oz) plain flour

50 g (2 oz) ginger biscuits, crushed or ground in a food processor

25 g (1 oz) porridge oats

100 g (3½ oz) unsalted butter or vegetarian margarine, plus extra for greasing

3 tablespoons light muscovado sugar

500 g (1 lb) rhubarb, chopped

2 tablespoons chopped preserved stem ginger, plus 2 tablespoons ginger syrup from jar

50 g (2 oz) caster sugar

4 tablespoons water

375 g (12 oz) dessert apples, peeled, cored and sliced

1 Sift the flour into a bowl and stir in the biscuits and oats. Rub in the butter or margarine until the mixture resembles breadcrumbs, then stir in the muscovado sugar.

2 Place the rhubarb in a saucepan with the ginger, ginger syrup, caster sugar and water. Heat gently, cover and simmer for 10 minutes.

3 Grease a pie dish and place the sliced apples in it. Add the rhubarb mixture and sprinkle over the crumble topping. Place in a preheated oven, 190°C (375°F) Gas Mark 5, for 40 minutes until the filling is bubbling and the topping golden. Serve hot.

**Serves 8**

**Preparation time:** 20 minutes

**Cooking time:** 50 minutes

# rhubarb, apple & double ginger crumble

# rum pancakes

1 Sift the flour into a bowl and make a well in the centre. Stir in the sugar, eggs, olive oil and rum. Mix well, drawing in the flour from the sides, until the mixture is smooth.

2 Gradually add the milk, a little at a time, beating well between each addition. The batter should be smooth and the consistency of single cream. Add a little more milk if necessary and then leave to stand for 1 hour.

3 Brush a small omelette pan with a little oil and heat thoroughly. Pour in sufficient batter to cover the base of the pan thinly, tilting the pan until evenly covered. Cook until the underside of the batter is set and golden brown, and then flip the pancake over and cook the other side. Remove and keep warm. Cook the remaining pancakes in the same way.

4 To make the filling, whip the cream until thick and gently stir in the rum and sugar. Spread the warm pancakes with the filling and roll up or fold over. Sprinkle with grated chocolate and serve immediately.

150 g (5 oz) plain flour

1 teaspoon sugar

2 eggs

1 tablespoon olive oil

1 tablespoon rum

300 ml (½ pint) milk

1 tablespoon vegetable oil

grated chocolate, to decorate

**Filling:**

300 ml (½ pint) double cream

2 tablespoons rum

2 teaspoons caster sugar

---

**Serves 4–6**

**Preparation time:** 10 minutes, plus standing

**Cooking time:** 10 minutes

# chilled fig soup

1 Set aside 4 of the figs. Place the other figs in a large saucepan with the remaining ingredients. Bring to the boil, reduce the heat and simmer for 2 minutes. Remove from the heat, cover and leave to marinate for 10 minutes.

2 Add the vanilla essence, cinnamon stick and orange rind to the soup. Process the soup in a blender or food processor, in batches if necessary. Strain through a sieve and return to the pan.

3 Add the reserved figs to the saucepan with the soup, bring to the boil, reduce the heat, cover and simmer for 5–7 minutes until tender, turning the figs over after 2–3 minutes. Transfer the poached figs and soup to a bowl, taste and add more honey or lemon juice if required. Cool, cover and chill thoroughly.

4 Just before serving, remove the figs with a slotted spoon and cut each one into wedges. Ladle the soup into chilled bowls and garnish with the fig wedges. Serve with the cattucini biscuits and a spoonful of mascarpone cheese.

16 small figs, preferably black

a few drops of vanilla essence

5 cm (2 inch) piece of cinnamon stick

2 strips of orange rind

250 ml (8 fl oz) water

375 ml (13 fl oz) red wine

2 tablespoons clear honey

2 tablespoons lemon juice

### To Serve:

cattucini or other Italian biscuits

4 tablespoons mascarpone cheese

### Serves 4

**Preparation time:** 15 minutes, plus chilling

**Cooking time:** 15 minutes

# orange tart

1 Put the flour into a bowl, add the butter or margarine and rub it in until the mixture resembles fine bread-crumbs. Stir in the sugar, then add the egg yolk. Mix to a firm dough, adding a little water if necessary.

2 Turn the dough out on to a lightly floured surface and knead briefly. Roll out and line a 20 cm (8 inch) deep flan tin. Chill for 30 minutes, then fill with crumpled foil and bake in a preheated oven, 200°C (400°F) Gas Mark 6, for 15 minutes. Remove the foil and cook the pastry case for 5 minutes more. Reduce the oven temperature to 160°C (325°F) Gas Mark 3.

3 Make the filling. Whisk the eggs, egg yolks and sugar in a bowl until foamy. Whisk in the cream. Grate the rind from the 3 oranges and squeeze the juice from 1 of them. Use the remaining oranges in another recipe. Add the rind and juice to the egg mixture and whisk again. Pour into the pastry case and bake for 30–35 minutes, until the filling is firm.

4 Prepare the decoration. Pare the rind from the orange; do not include any white pith. Cut the rind into thin strips. Place the sugar in a pan with the water. Bring to the boil, stirring until the sugar has dissolved. Add the rind and boil for 2–3 minutes without stirring, until syrupy. Using a slotted spoon, transfer the rind from the syrup to a plate. Whip the double cream until stiff and use it to decorate the rim of the tart. Sprinkle with the glazed orange rind and serve cold.

**Pastry:**

175 g (6 oz) plain flour

75 g (3 oz) chilled butter or vegetarian margarine, diced

50 g (2 oz) caster sugar

1 egg yolk

**Filling:**

2 eggs, plus 2 egg yolks

150 g (5 oz) caster sugar

150 ml (¼ pint) single cream

3 oranges

**To Decorate:**

1 orange

75 g (3 oz) caster sugar

3 tablespoons water

150 ml (¼ pint) double cream

**Serves 6**

**Preparation time:** 30 minutes

**Cooking time:** 50–55 minutes

1 Lightly grease a 30 x 23 cm (12 x 9 inch) shallow baking tin. To make the orange pastry, cream the butter or margarine, sugar and orange rind until light and fluffy. Gradually work in the flour until the mixture resembles fine breadcrumbs. Press the pastry firmly and evenly into the prepared tin.

2 Bake in a preheated oven, 190°C (375°F) Gas Mark 5, for 10 minutes. Remove from the oven. Reduce the heat to 180°C (350°F) Gas Mark 4.

3 Sift the flour and baking powder into a bowl. Cream the eggs and the brown sugar in a second bowl until well mixed. Blend in the vanilla and orange rind. Gradually beat in the flour mixture until well combined. Stir in the walnuts and coconut. Spread the mixture over the partially baked pastry and bake for 20–25 minutes or until well browned and set in the centre. Transfer the tin to a rack.

4 To make the orange glaze, mix the sugar and orange rind, then stir in the juice until the icing is smooth. Drizzle over the pastry while still warm. Leave the cake to stand until the glaze is set and then cut it into slices in the tin. Remove from the tin when cold.

25 g (1 oz) plain flour

½ teaspoon baking powder

2 eggs

250 g (8 oz) soft brown sugar

1 teaspoon vanilla essence

1 tablespoon grated orange rind

125 g (4 oz) shelled walnuts, chopped

140 g (4½ oz) desiccated coconut

**Orange Pastry:**

125 g (4 oz) butter or vegetarian margarine, softened, plus extra for greasing.

125 g (4 oz) sugar

1 teaspoon grated orange rind

125 g (4 oz) plain flour

**Orange Glaze:**

175 g (6 oz) icing sugar

1 teaspoon grated orange rind

1½ tablespoons orange juice

**Makes 36**

**Preparation time:** 25–35 minutes

**Cooking time:** 30–35 minutes

# double orange slices

# lemon soufflé pancakes

1 To make the batter, sift the flour into a mixing bowl. Make a well in the centre and add the egg and half the milk. Beat the liquid ingredients with a wooden spoon to mix, then gradually draw in the flour, stirring well. When the mixture is smooth, stir in the remaining milk. Cover and chill for 1–2 hours.

2 Lightly grease a 15 cm (6 inch) omelette pan and set over a medium heat. Pour in about 3 table-spoons of the batter and tilt and rotate the pan to coat the base evenly, then tip out any excess batter. Cook for 30–45 seconds until the pancake is just set and the underside is golden brown. Loosen the edge with a palette knife and turn or flip the pancake over. Cook the other side for 30 seconds, then slide out of the pan. Cook the remaining pancakes in the same way.

3 To make the filling, melt the butter or margarine in a saucepan, stir in the flour and cook for 2–3 minutes. Add the milk, sugar, lemon rind and juice. Bring to the boil, stirring until thickened. Cool slightly and beat in the egg yolks. Whisk the egg whites until stiff and fold in. Fill, fold and place the pancakes in an ovenproof dish. Dust with icing sugar. Bake in a preheated oven, 200°C (400°F) Gas Mark 6, for 10–15 minutes.

50 g (2 oz) plain flour

1 egg, beaten

200 ml (7 fl oz) milk

butter or vegetarian margarine for greasing

### Filling:

25 g (1 oz) butter or vegetarian margarine

25 g (1 oz) plain flour

300 ml (½ pint) milk

25 g (1 oz) caster sugar

grated rind and juice of 1 lemon

2 eggs, separated, plus 1 egg white

25 g (1 oz) icing sugar

**Makes 8**

**Preparation time:** 25 minutes, plus chilling

**Cooking time:** 30 minutes

# fresh lemon slices

1 Generously grease a 30 x 23 cm (12 x 9 inch) shallow baking tin. Put the butter or margarine, 50 g (2 oz) of the icing sugar and the vanilla essence into a bowl and beat until light and fluffy. Sift the flour and fold it, a little at a time, into the mixture until completely incorporated. Spread the mixture evenly in the prepared tin and bake in a preheated oven, 190°C (375°F), Gas Mark 5, for 20 minutes.

2 Meanwhile, put the eggs, sugar, lemon rind and lemon juice into a bowl. Stir to blend the ingredients but do not beat. Pour the mixture over the baked pastry layer. Return the tin to the oven and bake for 18–22 minutes until the topping is set and lightly browned.

3 Remove the tin from the oven and sift the remaining icing sugar over the cake to cover it generously. Cut the cake into slices. Remove from the tin when cool.

250 g (8 oz) butter or vegetarian margarine, softened, plus extra for greasing

75 g (3 oz) icing sugar

1 teaspoon vanilla essence

250 g (8 oz) plain flour

4 eggs

175 g (6 oz) sugar

grated rind of 1 lemon

6 tablespoons lemon juice

**Makes 36**

**Preparation time:** 15 minutes

**Cooking time:** 38–42 minutes

# index

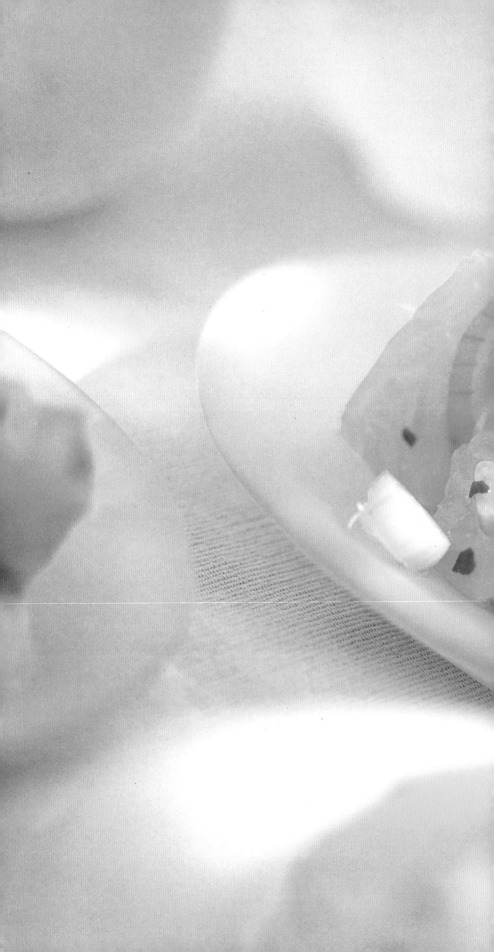